LEADER'S GUIDE

Living *in the* Excellence *of* Jesus!

Written by Cheryl Price, Ph.D.

Edited by Evangeline Carey

UMI (Urban Ministries, Inc.)
Chicago, Illinois

Publisher
UMI (Urban Ministries, Inc.)
P. O. Box 436987
Chicago, IL 60643-6987

First Edition
First Printing
ISBN-13: 978-1-934056-63-9
ISBN-10: 1-934056-63-4

1-800-860-8642
www.urbanministries.com

Copyright© 2007 by UMI. All rights reserved.

Scripture marked NLT are taken from the Holy Bible, New Living Translation, Copyright© 1996. Used by permission of Tyndale House Publishers, Inc., Wheaton, Illinois 60189. All rights reserved.

Scripture marked NIV are taken from the HOLY BIBLE, NEW INTERNATIONAL VERSION®. Copyright© 1973, 1978, 1984 by International Bible Society. Used by permission of Zondervan. All rights reserved.

No part of this publication may be reproduced, stored in a retrieval system, or transmitted in any form or by any means—electronic, mechanical, photocopy, recording, or otherwise—without written permission of the publisher of this book.

Printed in the United States of America.

Table of Contents

Introduction v

Chapter 1
Trusting God in the Unexpected 1

Chapter 2
If These Walls Could Talk 7

Chapter 3
When God Says "Yes"! 13

Chapter 4
Afraid, But Not Alone 19

Chapter 5
Jesus in Strange Places 25

Chapter 6
A Knee-Bent Healing 31

Chapter 7
An Expensive Meal 37

Chapter 8
Trouble in the Camp 43

Chapter 9
Working Hard or Hardly Working? 49

Chapter 10
ROI: A Return on Investment 55

Introduction

Jesus is God and He is excellent in all His ways. His Word tells us that humanity is made in the "image," or "likeness," of God (Genesis 1:26). This does not mean that we look like Him physically, because He is a Spirit. Instead, an all-knowing God has given us the ability and the power to reflect the "fruit" of His Spirit, which is "love, joy, peace, longsuffering, gentleness, goodness, faith, meekness, and temperance" (Galatians 5:22–23).

As the Psalm writer so eloquently wrote, "O Lord, our Lord, how excellent is thy name in all the earth. . ." (Psalm 8:1). What words of adoration and praise to the Lord! We too should sing, shout, and share with one another about the meaning of the excellence of the name of our magnificent God. When we think of the beauty of the earth, the blessings we have and give to others, and the grace and mercy that the Lord allows us each and every day, like the prophet Jeremiah, there should be a song in our hearts that wells up from the fire of the Lord within (Jeremiah 20:9). Have you experienced this fire from within that wants to burst through the inner chambers of your heart, and that cannot be contained until you tell someone else about Jesus and His excellence? Has God ever delivered you from a difficult or seemingly impossible situation or healed your broken heart? The Lord's transforming love, in unexpected or rock—hard place life moments, gives us the time to bask and rejoice in who God is and how much He cares for us. What a powerful revelation for each of us personally and collectively. We serve a God who loves us so much that He was willing to give His life, through Christ, to save us and He blesses us in spite of shortcomings, hesitations, or lack of honesty and faith. Jesus' death and Resurrection are transforming to all who accept, believe, and live His Word.

Living in the excellence of Jesus requires us to give our best and do our best even when we do not want to. Learning, receiving, and enjoying living in the excellence of Jesus are undergirded and wrapped up in the love of ". . .God that is revealed in Christ Jesus" (Romans 8:39, NLT). The love of God, through Jesus, gives hope and assurance that we can always try to do things in a more excellent way. When we try and when we fail, we have the love of Christ to guide us and deliver us from our failures and brush us off to start over again. When we succeed at choosing the way of excellence and help others to give their best, we have given a wonderful blessing from the Lord to others.

Living in the Excellence of Jesus! examines—through biblical and true-to-life accounts, illustrations, and statistics from this postmodern era—how we can walk in the Lord's footsteps with excellence. It embraces the fact that, as God grows the fruit of His Spirit in us, we learn to cultivate excellence in trust, faith, prayer, leadership, determination, hope, discipline, obedience, our work for God, and servanthood. Those who obey His Word will reap the rewards of righteous living promised by a God who is good and faithful (Revelation 22:12).

Introduction

Purpose of the Book. Living in the Excellence of Jesus! is a guide to encourage the biblical foundation truth that victory in life, regardless of the circumstances, is grounded in the faith and belief of who God is and how God moves in our lives. The lessons contained in this book are important tools to encourage readers to spend time thinking, sharing, and living in the Word.

Each of the chapters provides the leader with important information regarding an outline for each lesson and explanations to help the leader guide the students through the small and large discussions, leader's guide for discussions and beginning lessons, and practical teaching applications for the teacher.

Through studying Living in the Excellence of Jesus! discover how to "graduate to great" in your Christian walk with a Holy God.

Living in the Excellence of Jesus! is designed to help those who are interested in perfecting their walk with God by striving to be all that He is calling for them to be. It teaches that indeed the righteous have many struggles and problems, but God can use them to develop character that will glorify and honor Him.

Living in the Excellence of Jesus! adult curriculum is ideal for Vacation Bible School, Church School electives, church-wide retreats, book clubs, family-based or small group Bible studies, and personal enrichment.

As you study and teach Living in the Excellence of Jesus! we encourage you to have the following tools to equip your teaching and learning opportunities in and out of the classroom.
- Schedule prayer time before and after your class preparation.
- Read and study the background of the book from the Bible that you are teaching.
- Keep a notebook for new words or information that you researched and questions that you may want to ask the class.
- Read the entire chapter of the lesson you are studying and also the chapter before and after that particular lesson.
- Be open to learning and saying, "I don't know," but let us learn together.

Teaching Suggestions. Remember, everyone learns differently. How you learn affects how you teach.

Incorporate a variety of ways to learn in your lesson planning so that you will reach as many people as possible. Have students design plays, role-play, write poems, cook, or paint to serve as a way to introduce the lessons or as part of the lessons. If you are a first time teacher, talk with a seasoned teacher from church or in a school about some suggestions for creating opportunities for your lessons to come to life. Lecturing should not be the only way you communicate with the class.

Introduction

Small Groups are wonderful ways to engage the class to talk and share among themselves and report back to the larger group. Participants who are reserved may feel more comfortable talking in the smaller groups.

Large Groups give the class a chance to interact with the teacher serving as facilitator in many of the discussions so that more than one person is able to talk. Some of the activities you may decide at the beginning of the lesson may require the whole class to participate. The large group can provide a sense of accountability for everyone participating together to make something happen.

Enjoy teaching and take the time to praise the Lord while teaching. Meet with the other teachers for a time of prayer and a time of fellowship. Make some time to laugh and get to know each other away from the class location. This will help to create a bond between the teachers. Teaching is work and our work needs to be tempered with relaxation for ourselves as well. Take the time to care for yourself so that you will be refreshed and better prepared to teach and list.

The Leader's Guide. The leader's guide gives the facilitator, or instructor, a suggested lesson plan or "teaching tips" for teaching the class. Using the optional format discussed, the facilitator can utilize the student workbook questions or the questions at the end of each chapter in the student book either for classroom discussion, homework, or both. Each chapter of the guide contains:
- The Lesson Aim, which numerates what each student should learn from the lesson
- A Scripture Key Verse, which give the biblical perspective on the lesson
- A Lesson Focus, which tells the leader what the focus of the lesson should be on
- A Prayer section with suggestions for prayer, since each session should start and end with prayer
- An Introduction, which introduces what the lesson hopes to cover
- A Chapter Review, which introduces topics to be used in reviewing each chapter
- A Do You Know. . . ? section, which introduces words, phrases, and names you should know from the lesson
- An Up Front and Personal Discussion Questions section, which explains how to use the Up Front and Personal Discussion Questions
- A Small Group Strategies section, which explains what to do in the small group assembly
- A Clock Watchers section, which helps with time constraints
- A Meditate and Debate section, which encourages the small group to divide the questions and Scriptures among the members. Then they should spend time discussing the answers to the questions

Introduction

- A Summary Reports section, which explains how small groups are to do their summaries
- A Large Group Strategies section, which explains what to do in the large group assembly
- A Doer of the Word section, which explains how to apply God's principles to everyday living
- A Something to Think About... section, which gives the students a topic to think about and discuss
- A Closing section, which has reminders

Note: Answers to the questions in the student workbook are found in the leader's guide.

The Student Workbook. The student workbook accompanies the book *Living in the Excellence of Jesus!* Students should also be encouraged to get the student workbook because it will enhance their learning experience. It contains the following:
- The companion Key Verse, which should be memorized
- The Lesson Focus, an enhancer and reminder before doing the questions
- The Do You Know . . .? section, which consists of words, phrases, or names to enhance answering each question
- Questions and spaces for the answers from all sections of the book *Living in the Excellence of Jesus!* including: Up Front and Personal, A Word from the Lord, Something to Think About . . ., A Doer of the Word, and Prayer Forum.

Finally, use *Living in the Excellence of Jesus!* and its companion leader's guide and student workbook to help teach your participants the Word of God. Help them to see and understand how to apply His principles to their everyday living. Help them to grow in their knowledge of the God they serve, in their intimate relationship with Him, and in the excellence of Jesus.

Chapter 1

TRUSTING GOD IN THE UNEXPECTED

BASED ON LUKE 1:26–45

Format for Sessions of 90 Minutes or More

PART ONE

MIN.	ACTIVITY
5	Prayer
10	Introduction
15	Chapter Review
20	A Doer of the Word Discussion

PART TWO

MIN.	ACTIVITY
20	Small Group Strategies
15	Small Group Presentation
15	Large Group Presentation
5	Prayer Initiatives

To complete the group study in PART ONE and PART TWO, each participant will need a copy of the *Living in the Excellence of Jesus!* workbook that accompanies the student book. You may use PART ONE for sessions less than 90 minutes. Then, in the group settings, they will discuss their answers. Always close the sessions with prayer.

LESSON AIM: At the end of the one- or two-part session, the participants should: (1) know what it means to trust in the Living God; (2) be able to trust God in the unexpected situations that they face; (3) be able to minister to others in their times of need; and (4) find and know scriptural references on trusting God

KEY VERSE: *"Gabriel appeared to [Mary] and said, 'Greetings, favored woman! The Lord is with you'"* (Luke 1:28, NLT).

LESSON FOCUS: God sent the Savior of humanity, the Messiah Jesus, God's one and only Son, through a virgin. Her name was Mary. God favored Mary enough to trust her and her betrothed (fiance), Joseph—who was Jesus' legal father, but not His biological father—with such a precious seed. This favor of God was so unexpected. In addition, there were serious ramifications for Mary, being pregnant with this *Child of the Holy Spirit*, in her unmarried state. Both she and Joseph had to trust God in the unexpected.

CHAPTER 1

PART ONE

PRAYER
Always open the session with prayer and thanksgiving to God. Also include the Lesson Aim in your prayer.

INTRODUCTION
Introduce the chapter title and Scripture reference, including some background on the author of the book in which the Scripture is found, his audience, and his purpose for writing. (Note: Use a Bible Commentary, search online, or use your local library to get assistance). Then have a volunteer read the Key Verse aloud. It also appears at the beginning of each chapter in the student book. Now discuss the Key Verse and then have another volunteer read the Lesson Focus. Discuss. Finally introduce the vocabulary words or names and phrases listed in the Do You Know . . .? section, stressing their meaning.

CHAPTER REVIEW
After introducing the following topics, allow about five minutes to review and discuss Chapter 1.
- Why did humanity need a Savior?
- Why couldn't just any human save humanity?
- Who supplied the Savior?
- How does one become saved?

DO YOU KNOW. . . ?
To prepare for the lesson, study the following words and definitions (all are taken from Chapter 1—"Trusting God in the Unexpected").
ambiguous—confusing, vague, unclear, uncertain
barren—infertile, sterile
excellence—brilliance, distinction, fineness, superior
trust—confidence, conviction, dependence, faith, hope, reliance

UP FRONT AND PERSONAL DISCUSSION QUESTIONS
After introducing and discussing the Up Front and Personal section of the book, go to the Up Front and Personal Discussion Questions in the student workbook. The workbook has space provided to record answers. Again, encourage participants to answer the questions as homework. If not, allow time for them to do so in class. To facilitate discussion, you might read them aloud, allow the participants to share their answers, and also share your thoughts. Always refer to the Bible as the final authority.

PART TWO
SMALL GROUP STRATEGIES
Assemble Into Small Groups. Ask the participants to form small groups (tailor the number in each group to the size of the class). Assign each group a different section of the remaining parts of the chapter in the student book:
- Group #1   A Word from the Lord
- Group #2   Something to Think About. . .
- Group #3   A Doer of the Word

Also assign each group their respective sections in the student workbook (only A Word from the Lord and A Doer of the Word). Inform them that they are to complete and discuss the workbook questions for their respective section and report their answers to the larger group at the end of the study period.

Clock Watchers. Time constraints are very important in covering all the materials of the session. Therefore, approximately 15–20 minutes should be allotted for the Small Group Strategies.

Meditate and Debate. Encourage the small group to divide the questions and Scriptures among the members. Then, they should spend time discussing the answers to the questions.

Summary Reports. Each small group should prepare a summary of their session to share with the larger group by having a chairperson who will: (1) take notes; (2) summarize the discussion; and (3) present.

LARGE GROUP STRATEGIES
Reassemble. The groups should reassemble so that their findings can be discussed within the larger group.

Clock Watchers. Your objective is to cover all of the materials for each session. Therefore, allot two or three minutes for the small group spokespersons to give their summaries. In addition, allocate another two to three minutes to discuss the smaller groups' presentations.

A DOER OF THE WORD
Because it tells the participants how to apply God's Word to real-life situations, this is a very important part of your discussion. Therefore, summarize the salient points in this section and discuss them corporately.

Chapter 1

Something to Think About. . .
This question can be used for further discussion sessions. The participants may ask additional questions, and more time for dialogue may be needed. You may want to designate another time for the questions to be discussed as a part of your class in the future or at another group study gathering.

Closing
Remind the participants to read Chapter 2 of *Living in the Excellence of Jesus!* and complete the exercises assigned in the student workbook. Also encourage them to bring their Bibles to each session. Always close with prayer.

UP FRONT AND PERSONAL DISCUSSION QUESTIONS
The answers will vary.
1. Think of a nursery rhyme that you know and write it below. What do you think was the original intent or meaning of the nursery rhyme, and how is it understood today?

2. In our everyday life experiences, we use or say things that mean something different from its original meanings; however, today it has a new meaning or is obsolete. List three items as examples and share your thoughts with the class.

3. After reading the Up Front and Personal section, define *trust* in your own words.

4. Now, give an example of what it means to trust.

5. How does one trust God, whom he/she cannot see?

6. When should one trust God? Why?

7. How can you find or see the excellence of God in a situation that is characterized by both trauma and drama?

A WORD FROM THE LORD
The answers will vary.
1. Review the background information on Joseph, Mary, Zechariah, and Elizabeth. Then fill in the blanks with the names of some of your family members or close friends who are like family. Next, write three to four one-word descriptions about each person. Share with your class or small groups a funny or special story about a family member or friend that you listed.

CHAPTER 1

2. Mary's pregnancy, before the marriage ceremony was completed, would have caused her to be ostracized and possibly stoned to death. Do you think the customs then were fair to teenage mothers or teenage fathers? Think of some of the various ways churches have responded to teenage pregnancies. How do your church and society overall respond today to teenage pregnancies?

3. Elizabeth was an older woman and was thought to be cursed by God because she was barren. The stigma of being childless in their culture was very great. What is your understanding of how society and your particular family respond to women and men who are "childless"?

4. God always makes excellent choices as to who will carry out the Lord's work. Why do you think God chose Mary, a teenager, to be the mother of Jesus, and Joseph to be the legal father? If you were between the ages of 13–16, would God have been able to choose you to be the mother or father of Jesus? Why or why not?

5. Explain what Luke 1:26–45 teaches about "trust."

6. List some negative consequences of *not* trusting in God.

7. Paraphrase (state in your own words) and then personalize the following Scriptures on trust.
See the example for a:
a. Job 13:15, paraphrased: Job declares that even though God might kill him, he cannot wait to present his situation before God. Job knows that being a believer will save him in the long run. If he dies, he will be in the presence of God.
Personalized: In my suffering, God might kill me, but I am going to argue my case before the Living God. What will save me in the long run is that I have God in my life (I am saved). Without God in my life, I would be eternally separated from God.
b. Psalm 18:2, paraphrased and personalized
c. Proverbs 3:5, paraphrased and personalized
d. Isaiah 50:10, paraphrased and personalized

SOMETHING TO THINK ABOUT. . .
The answers will vary.

God's announcement of Mary's conception through the angel Gabriel is good news for Christians. To paraphrase an age-old question, is something good because it is good or because God said it is good? Explain your answer and give supportive information.

CHAPTER 1

A DOER OF THE WORD
The answers will vary.

1. When you look over your life now—your character (inward thoughts/feelings and outward expressions/actions), your relationship with Jesus and the church, your family, paid job/career choice, and your volunteer service—do you think you are living out, in all or some ways, what God originally meant for you to be and do? Why or why not? What can you do to make changes? Should you make changes?

2. What was the last crisis, or problem, that you faced? How did you work through the situation or how are you working through it? In addition to prayer, what other advice can you offer someone who is in a crisis?

3. List two major crisis areas in the African American community. Then share how your church works with other churches and community groups to address these issues.

4. Name at least one person who has provided you with assistance and/or affirmation during a difficult time in your life. Then, describe how you have assisted or given care to someone who was in a crisis or difficult situation. How did you feel during both of these experiences?

PRAYER FORUM
The answers will vary.

Write a prayer or words of inspiration for someone who has been impacted by a personal or natural disaster.

CHAPTER 2

IF THESE WALLS COULD TALK
(And I Bet They Would Say Something, Too!)

BASED ON JOSHUA 2:1–9, 12, 14–15

Format for Sessions of 90 Minutes or More

PART ONE

MIN.	ACTIVITY
5	Prayer
10	Introduction
15	Chapter Review
20	A Doer of the Word Discussion

PART TWO

MIN.	ACTIVITY
20	Small Group Strategies
15	Small Group Presentation
15	Large Group Presentation
5	Prayer Initiatives

To complete the group study in PART ONE and PART TWO, each participant will need a copy of the *Living in the Excellence of Jesus!* workbook that accompanies the student book. You may use PART ONE for sessions less than 90 minutes. Then, in the group settings, they will discuss their answers. Always close the sessions with prayer.

LESSON AIM: At the end of the one-or two-part session, the participants should: (1) know that even in the midst of suffering, a sovereign God is in control of His creation and never out of control; (2) know that God is a very present help in times of trouble; (3) appreciate that God still loves us, even in our suffering; and (4) know God can make our enemies fear us instead of us fearing them.

KEY VERSE: *"So the [two spies] set out and came to the house of a prostitute named Rahab and stayed there that night"* (Joshua 2:1, NLT).

LESSON FOCUS: Why would the two spies stop at the house of Rahab, who was a known prostitute? Was it because it was an ideal place for a quick escape in case they were discovered by the authorities? Or was it because it was a good place to gather important information, and certainly they needed to know all about their enemies? Or could it be that an all-knowing, all-seeing God directed them to go to Rahab's house because God had a plan for the salvation of humanity, and He was going to include Rahab in the lineage of Jesus Christ, the Savior? If these walls could talk, they would indeed have a story to tell.

Chapter 2

PART ONE

Prayer
Always open the session with prayer and thanksgiving to God. Also include the Lesson Aim in your prayer.

Introduction
Introduce the chapter title and Scripture reference, including some background on the author of the book in which the Scripture is found, his audience, and his purpose for writing. (Note: Use a Bible Commentary, search online, or use your local library to get assistance). Then, have a volunteer read the Key Verse aloud. It also appears at the beginning of each chapter in the student book. Now discuss the Key Verse and then have another volunteer read the Lesson Focus. Discuss. Finally introduce the vocabulary words or names and phrases listed in the Do You Know . . .? section, stressing their meaning.

Chapter Review
After introducing the following topics, allow about five minutes to review and discuss Chapter 2.
- Who is God?
- Who is Jesus?
- Why does God use "peculiar" people to forward His agenda?
- Why does God not need millions to fight against His enemies?

Do You Know . . .?
To prepare for the lesson, study the following words and definitions (all are taken from Chapter 2—"If These Walls Could Talk").
community of faith—the collection of believers, the church
faith—assurance, confidence, conviction, reliance, trust
institutionalized slavery—businesses and other institutions have built-in rules and regulations that help them discriminate against or bypass certain racial and ethnic groups in hiring, job promotions, etc.
pandemic—catastrophic events that destroy many lives (HIV/AIDS, storms, tornadoes, etc.)
sin—a willful breaking of God's laws or rules

Up Front and Personal Discussion Questions
After introducing and discussing the Up Front and Personal section of the book, go to the Up Front and Personal Discussion Questions in the student workbook. The workbook has space provided to record answers. Again, encourage participants to answer the questions as homework. If not, allow time for them to do so in class. To facilitate discussion, you might have them read aloud, allow the participants to share their answers, and also share your thoughts. Always refer to the Bible as the final authority.

PART TWO
SMALL GROUP STRATEGIES
Assemble Into Small Groups. Ask the participants to form small groups (tailor the number in each group to the size of the class). Assign each group a different section of the remaining parts of the chapter in the student book:
- Group #1   A Word from the Lord
- Group #2   Something to Think About. . .
- Group #3   A Doer of the Word

Also assign each group their respective sections in the student workbook (only A Word from the Lord and A Doer of the Word). Inform them that they are to complete and discuss the workbook questions for their respective section and report their answers to the larger group at the end of the study period.

Clock Watchers. Time constraints are very important in covering all the materials of the session. Therefore, approximately 15–20 minutes should be allotted for the Small Group Strategies.

Meditate and Debate. Encourage the small group to divide the questions and Scriptures among the members. Then, they should spend time discussing the answers to the questions.

Summary Reports. Each small group should prepare a summary of their session to share with the larger group by having a chairperson who will: (1) take notes; (2) summarize the discussion; and (3) present.

LARGE GROUP STRATEGIES
Reassemble. The groups should reassemble so that their findings can be discussed within the larger group.

Clock Watchers. Your objective is to cover all the materials for each session. Therefore, allot two or three minutes for the small group spokespersons to give their summaries. In addition, allocate another two to three minutes to discuss the smaller groups' presentations.

A DOER OF THE WORD
Because it tells the participants how to apply God's Word to real-life situations, this is a very important part of your discussion. Therefore, summarize the salient points in this section and discuss them corporately.

SOMETHING TO THINK ABOUT. . .
These statements and questions can be used for further discussion sessions. The

participants may ask additional questions, and more time for dialogue may be needed. You may want to designate another time for the questions to be discussed as a part of your class in the future or at another group study gathering.

Closing
Remind the participants to read Chapter 3 of *Living in the Excellence of Jesus!* and complete the exercises assigned in the student workbook. Also encourage them to bring their Bibles to each session. Always close with prayer.

UP FRONT AND PERSONAL DISCUSSION QUESTIONS
The answers will vary.

1. Discuss how you think you would feel (or would have felt) if you were taking a trip to the slave castles.

2. Name seven countries in Africa and describe something you know about each of them.

3. What sites in Africa would you like to visit and why? Is there any history that you want to share about your particular destination?

4. Name three slave revolt leaders. Do you think you would have escaped or assisted with the escape?

5. After reading the Up Front and Personal section, define *faith* in your own words.

6. Now, give an example of what it means to have faith in God in the midst of great suffering.

7. How can you find or see the excellence of God in the Up Front and Personal account of the slave castles? Where was God in all that suffering?

A WORD FROM THE LORD
The answers will vary.

1. What are some of the characteristics of Rahab and the spies that we can use in our lives to help deliver us in our problems?

2. List three assessments of Joshua and his leadership skills.

3. Who are the strong leaders in your church and why?

4. Name two attributes that make a great leader.

5. We all must follow someone at some point in our lives. Do you agree or disagree? Are you a leader or a follower? If you are considered a leader or a follower by others, what makes you either one or both?

6. Explain how you will implement at least three practical applications from this lesson into your life.

7. Paraphrase (state in your own words) and personalize the following Scriptures on faith.
   a. Matthew 9:22, paraphrased and personalized
   b. Luke 12:28, paraphrased and personalizedd
   c. John 3:16, paraphrased and personalized.

SOMETHING TO THINK ABOUT. . .
The answers will vary.
1. Name two of the Important persons listed in this section. Describe how you think their accomplishments have impacted the African American community and the world at-large.

2. Discuss the effects of drug abuse within the African American population and its impact within our country. What are the responses to the drug problem from your church's perspective, and is this response enough?

3. Why is the jail rate for African Americans so high, and what are the social and cultural implications for this epidemic? Share how you personally and your church collectively address the prison population problem for African Americans.

A DOER OF THE WORD
The answers will vary.
1. Although we may not choose certain people to do particular duties for the Lord, discuss the reasons you think God chooses people that we would consider the outcasts of society.

2. How effective is prayer without action in making changes to bring about a positive and healthy community for African Americans? What are some actions, in addition to prayer, that African Americans need to build a better community?

3. What are some of the destructive forces within the African American community? What are some of the positive forces?

PRAYER FORUM
The answers will vary.
>Write a prayer or words of inspiration that address destructive fear in our lives.

CHAPTER 3

WHEN GOD SAYS, "YES"!

BASED ON ACTS 12:5–17

Format for Sessions of 90 Minutes or More

PART ONE

MIN.	ACTIVITY
5	Prayer
10	Introduction
15	Chapter Review
20	A Doer of the Word Discussion

PART TWO

MIN.	ACTIVITY
20	Small Group Strategies
15	Small Group Presentation
15	Large Group Presentation
5	Prayer Initiatives

To complete the group study in PART ONE and PART TWO, each participant will need a copy of the *Living in the Excellence of Jesus!* workbook that accompanies the student book. You may use PART ONE for sessions less than 90 minutes. Then, in the group settings, they will discuss their answers. Always close the sessions with prayer.

LESSON AIM: At the end of the one- or two-part session, the participants should: (1) know our Heavenly Father is a loving Father and He does care about our needs and knows them well; (2) know that He hears us when we pray and He answers; (3) know that sometimes He says "no" or "wait"; and (4) know that He often says, "yes" to our requests so we should always pray with expectancy.

KEY VERSE: *"Suddenly, there was a bright light in the cell, and an angel of the Lord stood before Peter. The angel tapped him on the side to awaken him and said, 'Quick! Get up!' And the chains fell off his wrists"* (Acts 12:7, NLT).

LESSON FOCUS: When we take our requests before our loving Heavenly Father, we should go expecting Him to answer. We should go pregnant with hope to Almighty God to meet our daily needs. In today's Scriptures, when the church prayed for Peter, while he was in prison, God answered their prayers so quickly that it caught Peter and them by surprise. Needless to say, they were not expecting Him to say, "yes." This was shown by their surprise at finding Peter delivered and standing at the door. When we go to God with our earnest petitions, do we expect Him to say, "yes"?

PART ONE
Prayer
Always open the session with prayer and thanksgiving to God. Also include the Lesson Aim in your prayer.

Introduction
Introduce the chapter title and Scripture reference, including some background on the author of the book in which the Scripture is found, his audience, and his purpose for writing. (Note: Use a Bible Commentary, search online, or use your local library to get assistance). Then, have a volunteer read the Key Verse aloud. It also appears at the beginning of each chapter in the student book. Now discuss the Key Verse and then have another volunteer read the Lesson Focus. Discuss. Finally introduce the vocabulary words or names and phrases listed in the Do You Know . . .? section, stressing their meaning.

Chapter Review
After introducing the following topics, allow about five minutes to review and discuss Chapter 3.
- What is your response when God says, "no" to your request?
- What is your response when God says, "wait" to your request?
- What is your response when God says, "yes" to your request?
- Do you expect Him to say, "yes" to your request?

Do You Know. . . ?
To prepare for the lesson, study the following words and definitions (all are taken from Chapter 3—"When God Says, 'Yes'!").
a willing heart—an obedient heart to God's will and commands
an angel of the Lord—a messenger sent by God
giving God the victory—giving God the praises and glory for what He has done in our lives, is doing, and will do, based on His Word
God's favor—God's unmerited mercy and blessings upon our lives
Paul—the apostle who once persecuted the church, met Jesus on the Damascus Road, got saved, witnessed for Him by helping to establish many churches, and wrote many letters to these infant churches when they were in trouble; his letters make up much of the New Testament
the Last Supper—the dinner that Jesus had with His disciples in the Upper Room before His crucifixion
the Passover meal—the meal the Jews had in celebration of the time in Egypt when Jesus spared their firstborns from death and killed all of the Egyptians' firstborn because Pharaoh would not set the Israelites free from more than 400 years of slavery
to pray very earnestly—with trust, to sincerely petition God for our needs

Up Front and Personal Discussion Questions

After introducing and discussing the Up Front and Personal section of the book, go to the Up Front and Personal Discussion Questions in the student workbook. The workbook has space provided to record answers. Again, encourage participants to answer the questions as homework. If not, allow time for them to do so in class. To facilitate discussion, you might read them aloud, allow the participants to share their answers, and also share your thoughts. Always refer to the Bible as the final authority.

PART TWO
Small Group Strategies

Assemble Into Small Groups. Ask the participants to form small groups (tailor the number in each group to the size of the class). Assign each group a different section of the remaining parts of the chapter in the student book:

- Group #1   A Word from the Lord
- Group #2   Something to Think About...
- Group #3   A Doer of the Word

Also assign each group their respective sections in the student workbook (only A Word from the Lord and A Doer of the Word). Inform them that they are to complete and discuss the workbook questions for their respective section and report their answers to the larger group at the end of the study period.

Clock Watchers. Time constraints are very important in covering all the materials of the session. Therefore, approximately 15–20 minutes should be allotted for the Small Group Strategies.

Meditate and Debate. Encourage the small group to divide the questions and Scriptures among the members. Then, they should spend time discussing the answers to the questions.

Summary Reports. Each small group should prepare a summary of their session to share with the larger group by having a chairperson who will: (1) take notes; (2) summarize the discussion; and (3) present.

Large Group Strategies

Reassemble. The groups should reassemble so that their findings can be discussed within the larger group.

Clock Watchers. Your objective is to cover all of the materials for each session. Therefore, allot two or three minutes for the small group spokespersons to give their summaries. In addition, allocate another two to three minutes to discuss the smaller groups' presentations.

CHAPTER 3

A Doer of the Word
Because it tells the participants how to apply God's Word to real-life situations, this is a very important part of your discussion. Therefore, summarize the salient points in this section and discuss them corporately.

Something to Think About. . .
These questions can be used for further discussion sessions. The participants may ask additional questions, and more time for dialogue may be needed. You may want to designate another time for the questions to be discussed as a part of your class in the future or at another group study gathering.

Closing
Remind the participants to read Chapter 4 of *Living in the Excellence of Jesus!* and complete the exercises assigned in the student workbook. Also encourage them to bring their Bibles to each session. Always close with prayer.

UP FRONT AND PERSONAL DISCUSSION QUESTIONS
The answers will vary.

1. Anticipation and expectation can make us feel anxious and worried about whatever problems we are working on or working through. Share a time when you were waiting for a blessing and/or a breakthrough.

2. Is your nature more like D. King's or Debbie's? Why?

3. Briefly describe your reactions and listening level when someone else is waiting on a blessing or breakthrough.

4. List three Scriptures to help you and others work through their anticipations and anxieties while they are waiting to hear from God.

5. When was the last time you gave up on God blessing you as you worked through your breakthrough? Why did you give up and what was your response after "God showed up"?

A WORD FROM THE LORD
The answers will vary.

1. Describe the Jewish celebration of Passover and share how Passover is or is not celebrated within Christianity.

2. Why should Christians celebrate or not celebrate Passover?

3. Are there any celebrations that are similar to Passover within the African American church? List and explain.

4. Share what you know about the disciple Peter.

5. Do you have "Peter" qualities? If so, which ones?

6. Is it a benefit or a blessing for you and for building the kingdom of God on Earth to have some of Peter's qualities?

7. Why do you think John Mark's mother's home was the gathering place for the prayer service? Would your home be thought of as a place of prayer? Why? Why not?

8. Paraphrase (state in your own words) and then personalize the following Scriptures on prayer.
   a. Matthew 26:41, paraphrased and personalized
   b. Luke 11:1, paraphrased and personalized
   c. Romans 8:26, paraphrased and personalized
   d. Philippians 4:6, paraphrased and personalized

SOMETHING TO THINK ABOUT. . .
The answers will vary.

1. Waiting on God's response requires patience on our part. How do you help yourself be patient with God? How do you help others develop a more patient attitude with God?

2. Why do you think Jesus did not heal everyone or assist everyone with a need? What are the ways that your church responds to the various needs within the church, the community, and the world? What are some of the ministries that your church can focus on and do for others with your assistance?

3. Does your church have a Watch Night Service? What are the reasons and the rituals your church celebrates Watch Night Service?

4. Are there different rituals that you would like to include in the Watch Night Service?

A DOER OF THE WORD
The answers will vary.

1. What are some of the ways that your church uplifts the power of prayer? Explain.

2. How can you practice not worrying and trusting God in your times of need?

3. Describe your prayer life in times of difficulty and in good times. How do you share your experiences to help others who are going through difficult times and to encourage those who are not struggling to pray even in the good times?

4. If there is a prison ministry in your church, what are the responsibilities and how can you assist?

PRAYER FORUM
The answers will vary.
>Write a prayer below or words of inspiration thanking God for all He's done for you.

CHAPTER 4

AFRAID, BUT NOT ALONE

BASED ON JUDGES 4:4–16

Format for Sessions of 90 Minutes or More

PART ONE

MIN.	ACTIVITY
5	Prayer
10	Introduction
15	Chapter Review
20	A Doer of the Word Discussion

PART TWO

MIN.	ACTIVITY
20	Small Group Strategies
15	Small Group Presentation
15	Large Group Presentation
5	Prayer Initiatives

To complete the group study in PART ONE and PART TWO, each participant will need a copy of the *Living in the Excellence of Jesus!* workbook that accompanies the student book. You may use PART ONE for sessions less than 90 minutes. Then, in the group settings, they will discuss their answers. Always close the sessions with prayer.

LESSON AIM: At the end of the one- or two-part session, the participants should: (1) know that Almighty God is with us in our everyday struggles; (2) know we can trust Him to never leave or forsake us; (3) know we can trust Him to hear us when we pray; and (4) know we can trust Him to go before us and prepare and lead the way in battles with our enemies, including Satan.

KEY VERSE: *"Then Deborah said to Barak, 'Get ready! This is the day the LORD will give you victory over Sisera, for the LORD is marching ahead of you.' So Barak led his 10,000 warriors down the slopes of Mount Tabor into battle"* (Judges 4:14, NLT).

LESSON FOCUS: Barak, Israel's military leader, whose name means "thunderbolt," had been given a mission by God through Deborah, a prophetess and judge. God wanted him to lead the battle against King Jabin, who was a major enemy of God's chosen people, the Israelites. A man named Sisera led King Jabin of Hazor's army. They had 900 chariots of iron. When this "mighty" soldier, Barak, looked at the battle strategies with human eyes, instead of the fact that an all-powerful God was going before him to prepare the way, he became afraid. Therefore, he would not go into battle without Deborah by his side. This lesson will focus on trusting in Almighty God (having faith) when our fears try to win the day.

Chapter 4

PART ONE

Prayer
Always open the session with prayer and thanksgiving to God. Also include the Lesson Aim in your prayer.

Introduction
Introduce the chapter title and Scripture reference, including some background on the author of the book in which the Scripture is found, his audience, and his purpose for writing. (Note: Use a Bible Commentary, search online, or use your local library to get assistance). Then have a volunteer read the Key Verse aloud. It also appears at the beginning of each chapter in the student book. Now discuss the Key Verse and then have another volunteer read the Lesson Focus. Discuss. Finally introduce the vocabulary words or names and phrases listed in the Do You Know . . .? section, stressing their meaning.

Chapter Review
After introducing the following topics, allow about five minutes to review and discuss Chapter 4.
- When is fear a very real adversary?
- How should we deal with our fears?
- Where is God when we are afraid?
- How can trusting in God conquer fear?

Do You Know. . . ?
To prepare for the lesson, study the following names, phrases, and definitions. Match the words to the phrases that describe them (all are taken from Chapter 4—"Afraid, But Not Alone").

1. Barak
2. Deborah
3. Heber
4. Kedesh
5. King Jabin
6. Lappidoth
7. Naphtali
8. Sisera
9. the palm of Deborah
10. the Kishon River

a. commander of King Jabin's army
b. one of the 12 tribes of Israel
c. where Deborah lured Sisera and his troops
d. where Judge Deborah held court
e. commander of Israel's army
f. where Barak called together the tribes of Zebulun and Naphtali
g. prophetess and judge of Israel
h. a descendant of Hobab, Moses' brother-in-law
i. Deborah's husband
j. the king of Hazor, Israel's enemy

Chapter 4

Answers:

1. e
2. g
3. h
4. f
5. j

6. i
7. b
8. a
9. d
10. c

Up Front and Personal Discussion Questions

After introducing and discussing the Up Front and Personal section of the book, go to the Up Front and Personal Discussion Questions in the student workbook. The workbook has space provided to record answers. Again, encourage participants to answer the questions as homework. If not, allow time for them to do so in class. To facilitate discussion, you might read them aloud, allow the participants to share their answers, and also share your thoughts. Always refer to the Bible as the final authority

PART TWO

Small Group Strategies

Assemble Into Small Groups. Ask the participants to form small groups (tailor the number in each group to the size of the class). Assign each group a different section of the remaining parts of the chapter in the student book:

- Group #1   A Word from the Lord
- Group #2   Something to Think About. . .
- Group #3   A Doer of the Word

Also assign each group their respective sections in the student workbook (only A Word from the Lord and A Doer of the Word). Inform them that they are to complete and discuss the workbook questions for their respective section and report their answers to the larger group at the end of the study period.

Clock Watchers. Time constraints are very important in covering all the materials of the session. Therefore, approximately 15–20 minutes should be allotted for the Small Group Strategies.

Meditate and Debate. Encourage the small group to divide the questions and Scriptures among the members. Then, they should spend time discussing the answers to the questions.

Summary Reports. Each small group should prepare a summary of their session to share with the larger group by having a chairperson who will: (1) take notes; (2) summarize the discussion; and (3) present.

Large Group Strategies
Reassemble. The groups should reassemble so that their findings can be discussed within the larger group.

Clock Watchers. Your objective is to cover all of the materials for each session. Therefore, allot two or three minutes for the small group spokespersons to give their summaries. In addition, allocate another two to three minutes to discuss the smaller groups' presentations.

A Doer of the Word
Because it tells the participants how to apply God's Word to real-life situations, this is a very important part of your discussion. Therefore, summarize the salient points in this section and discuss them corporately.

Something to Think About. . .
These questions can be used for further discussion sessions. The participants may ask additional questions, and more time for dialogue may be needed. You may want to designate another time for the questions to be discussed as a part of your class in the future or at another group study gathering.

Closing
Remind the participants to read Chapter 5 of *Living in the Excellence of Jesus!* and complete the exercises assigned in the student workbook. Also encourage them to bring their Bibles to each session. Always close with prayer.

UP FRONT AND PERSONAL DISCUSSION QUESTIONS
The answers will vary.
1. Is there one or a few family members who have the responsibility to care for your family in various ways? Are you comfortable with this? Does it need to be changed? What can you do to make changes to this system?

2. Share a time when you or someone in your family had to make a major sacrifice for your family.

3. When feeling excluded, family members have ways to hold other members emotionally hostage for what they did to help someone else in the family. Share an account that you have witnessed or have heard about.

A WORD FROM THE LORD
The answers will vary.

CHAPTER 4

1. Why would Barak depend on Deborah instead of God?

2. Imagine and share how Deborah felt when Barak did not want to trust God's Word to him, and what Barak must have felt when he lacked the courage to go into battle without Deborah?

3. What can men learn from Barak about following the leadership of women?

4. What can women learn from Deborah about leadership and communication with God?

5. What can we learn from the biblical account of Deborah and Barak about fighting in spiritual warfare?

6. Paraphrase (state in your own words) and then personalize the following Scriptures on faith.
   a. Matthew 17:20, paraphrased and personalized
   b. Luke 18:42, paraphrased and personalized
   c. Ephesians 6:16, paraphrased and personalized

SOMETHING TO THINK ABOUT. . .
The answers will vary.

1. In biblical times, why do you think it was a disgrace for a soldier to be killed by a woman?

2. In today's society, do you think that there is too much emphasis placed on boys and men being stronger, and girls and women being weaker? Why or why not? Is it acceptable within our society for men to show fear greater than women or vice versa? Give examples to support your beliefs.

3. Discuss ways that we are to be humble before God, and why fear can be beneficial as well as detrimental.

A DOER OF THE WORD
The answers will vary.

1. Name two people whom you can depend on to give you support when you are afraid or feel alone.

2. Can others depend on you for support when they are feeling afraid or alone? Share how you show that you are dependable to those who need you in a crisis or just support them with your presence or kind words.

CHAPTER 4

PRAYER FORUM
The answers will vary.
> Write a prayer or words of inspiration that address the impact of God helping you in your spiritual battles.

CHAPTER 5

JESUS IN STRANGE PLACES

BASED ON LUKE 19:1–10

Format for Sessions of 90 Minutes or More

PART ONE

MIN.	ACTIVITY
5	Prayer
10	Introduction
15	Chapter Review
20	A Doer of the Word Discussion

PART TWO

MIN.	ACTIVITY
20	Small Group Strategies
15	Small Group Presentation
15	Large Group Presentation
5	Prayer Initiatives

To complete the group study in PART ONE and PART TWO, each participant will need a copy of the *Living in the Excellence of Jesus!* workbook that accompanies the student book. You may use PART ONE for sessions less than 90 minutes. Then, in the group settings, they will discuss their answers. Always close the sessions with prayer.

LESSON AIM: At the end of the one- or two-part session, the participants should: (1) appreciate that God can use "imperfect" people to do extraordinary things to help Him build His kingdom; (2) learn that spirituality can be real messy, but God expects believers to be lights in a dark world of sin; (3) know that God's agenda is saving lost souls; and (4) be reminded again that God saves from the "guttermost" to the uttermost.

KEY VERSE: *"Jesus responded, 'Salvation has come to this home today, for this man has shown himself to be a true son of Abraham'"* (Luke 19:9, NLT).

LESSON FOCUS: This lesson focuses on God's agenda and His ability to seek and save the spiritually lost, no matter who they are or where they may be. He sent His one and only Son (Jesus) to save the lost—those who needed a Savior.

PART ONE

PRAYER
Always open the session with prayer and thanksgiving to God. Also include the Lesson Aim in your prayer.

INTRODUCTION
Introduce the chapter title and Scripture reference, including some background on the author of the book in which the Scripture is found, his audience, and his purpose for writing. (Note: Use a Bible Commentary, search online, or use your local library to get assistance). Then have a volunteer read the Key Verse aloud. It also appears at the beginning of each chapter in the student book. Now discuss the Key Verse and then have another volunteer read the Lesson Focus. Discuss. Finally introduce the vocabulary words or names and phrases listed in the Do You Know . . .? section, stressing their meaning.

CHAPTER REVIEW
After introducing the following topics, allow about five minutes to review and discuss Chapter 5.
- Why does God choose to save whomever He wishes?
- What would happen if God allowed believers to choose who would be saved?
- What are some of the strange places that you have seen Jesus?

DO YOU KNOW. . . ?
To prepare for the lesson, study the following words and definitions (all are taken from Chapter 5—"Jesus in Strange Places").

a. Abraham
b. Jericho
c. Man
d. notorious sinner
e. sycamore
f. tax collector

1. Jesus met Zacchaeus in the city of _____ (Luke 19:1).
2. Zacchaeus was a _____ (his occupation) (v. 2).
3. Zacchaeus climbed in a _____ tree to see Jesus (v. 4).
4. Zacchaeus was considered to be a _____ _____ by the rest of the Jews (v. 7).
5. Zacchaeus showed himself to be a son of _____ (v. 9).
6. Jesus, the Son of _____, came to seek and save the spiritually lost (v. 10).

ANSWERS:
1. b
2. f
3. e
4. d
5. a
6. c

CHAPTER 5

UP FRONT AND PERSONAL DISCUSSION QUESTIONS
After introducing and discussing the Up Front and Personal section of the book, go to the Up Front and Personal Discussion Questions in the student workbook. The workbook has space provided to record answers. Again, encourage participants to answer the questions as homework. If not, allow time for them to do so in class. To facilitate discussion, you might read them aloud, allow the participants to share their answers, and also share your thoughts. Always refer to the Bible as the final authority.

PART TWO
SMALL GROUP STRATEGIES
Assemble Into Small Groups. Ask the participants to form small groups (tailor the number in each group to the size of the class). Assign each group a different section of the remaining parts of the chapter in the student book:
- Group #1   A Word from the Lord
- Group #2   Something to Think About. . .
- Group #3   A Doer of the Word

Also assign each group their respective sections in the student workbook (only A Word from the Lord and A Doer of the Word). Inform them that they are to complete and discuss the workbook questions for their respective section and report their answers to the larger group at the end of the study period.

Clock Watchers. Time constraints are very important in covering all the materials of the session. Therefore, approximately 15–20 minutes should be allotted for the Small Group Strategies.

Meditate and Debate. Encourage the small group to divide the questions and Scriptures among the members. Then, they should spend time discussing the answers to the questions.

Summary Reports. Each small group should prepare a summary of their session to share with the larger group by having a chairperson who will: (1) take notes; (2) summarize the discussion; and (3) present.

LARGE GROUP STRATEGIES
Reassemble. The groups should reassemble so that their findings can be discussed within the larger group.

Clock Watchers. Your objective is to cover all of the materials for each session. Therefore, allot two or three minutes for the small group spokespersons to give their

A Doer of the Word
Because it tells the participants how to apply God's Word to real-life situations, this is a very important part of your discussion. Therefore, summarize the salient points in this section and discuss them corporately.

Something to Think About. . .
These questions can be used for further discussion sessions. The participants may ask additional questions, and more time for dialogue may be needed. You may want to designate another time for the questions to be discussed as a part of your class in the future or at another group study gathering.

Closing
Remind the participants to read Chapter 6 of *Living in the Excellence of Jesus!* and complete the exercises assigned in the student workbook. Also encourage them to bring their Bibles to each session. Always close with prayer.

UP FRONT AND PERSONAL DISCUSSION QUESTIONS
The answers will vary.

1. What is your definition of "spirituality" and "spiritual"?

2. Name some of the rituals that you practice to develop your spiritual life.

3. Who has Jesus shown favor to that you are willing to admit you were either surprised about or did not think they deserved the blessing? Explain.

4. When was the last time you wanted to see Jesus in your life with the enthusiasm of Zacchaeus?

5. Share the time when you truly felt sorry for your sin, so you gave back to others or gave extra special blessings to others.

6. Why is society often cruel to those who are considered "odd" or "imperfect"?

7. Why do you think that God chooses "imperfect" people as vessels He can use to help build His kingdom?

CHAPTER 5

A WORD FROM THE LORD
The answers will vary.

1. Name two individuals that represent Zacchaeus in your life and what makes them like Zacchaeus.

2. From what you have read about Zacchaeus, did the other Jews have a right to hate him so much? Why?

3. When is being a tax collector a noble profession?

4. In your own words, why was Zacchaeus so desperate to see Jesus?

5. Did Zacchaeus have a right to see Jesus? Why?

6. Did the rest of the Jews really know who Jesus was and His purpose for coming into this world? Explain.

7. Paraphrase (state in your own words) and then personalize the following Scriptures on faith.
   a. 1 Chronicles 17:18, paraphrased and personalized
   b. Psalm 69:5, paraphrased and personalized
   c. Psalm 139:1–2, paraphrased and personalized

SOMETHING TO THINK ABOUT. . .
The answers will vary.

1. What is bullying?

2. Do you see any differences between bullying today and when you were growing up?

3. Share your thoughts on why the Good Samaritan and the woman who gave all her money did their best. What can we learn from them about a Christian's understanding of helping others who are in need regardless of our circumstances?

4. What programs and people in your church represent the transformed Zacchaeus? How can these programs be enhanced to reach others, and what can church members learn from the people who have a Zacchaeus spirit?

A DOER OF THE WORD
The answers will vary.

1. Describe a time that you were picked on or talked about someone (out loud or secretly) who was odd or different from the group. Maybe they did not agree with the group about an idea or dressed in a strange way. As a believer, what should you have done?

2. Describe how your church deals with people who are different from the norm of the congregation.

3. Were you ever bullied in your life? How did you handle it? If you were a bully, why did you act this way?

4. When people are bullied, they can believe that they are helpless victims. As believers, how should we respond to people who feel this way?

5. What would Jesus have us do to encourage living in His excellence and not in the shadows of the bullies at church, at work, in school, at home, etc.?

6. Explain how you will implement at least three practical applications from this lesson into your life.

7. List the areas in your life that need to be nurtured and encouraged to grow as you work toward the excellence that God has placed within you. If you do not have areas in your life that are underdeveloped, how are you helping someone else to be the best that he/she can be (but not as your clone)?

PRAYER FORUM
The answers will vary.

Write a prayer or words of inspiration that ask for help in the areas in your life that need changing so that you can be all that God is calling for you to be.

CHAPTER 6

A KNEE-BENT HEALING

BASED ON MARK 5:25–34

Format for Sessions of 90 Minutes or More

PART ONE

MIN.	ACTIVITY
5	Prayer
10	Introduction
15	Chapter Review
20	A Doer of the Word Discussion

PART TWO

MIN.	ACTIVITY
20	Small Group Strategies
15	Small Group Presentation
15	Large Group Presentation
5	Prayer Initiatives

To complete the group study in PART ONE and PART TWO, each participant will need a copy of the *Living in the Excellence of Jesus!* workbook that accompanies the student book. You may use PART ONE for sessions less than 90 minutes. Then, in the group settings, they will discuss their answers. Always close the sessions with prayer.

LESSON AIM: At the end of the one- or two-part session, the participants should: (1) know that desperate situations call for an Almighty God (a God who is more than enough in our times of need); (2) appreciate that God loves them and cares about their needs; (3) know that when life drives them to their knees, they can look up to a Mighty God; and (4) know that there is nothing too hard for Almighty God.

KEY VERSE: *"For [the sick woman] thought to herself, 'If I can just touch his robe, I will be healed'"* (Mark 5:28, NLT).

LESSON FOCUS: Life sometimes deals us a desperate hand. After all, even though this fallen world is not our permanent home, we are still in the world. Plus, believers are in spiritual warfare. Ephesians 6:10–12 (NLT) instructs us to, "Be strong in the Lord and in his mighty power. Put on all of God's armor so that you will be able to stand firm against all strategies and tricks of the devil. For we are not fighting against flesh-and-blood enemies, but against evil rulers and authorities of the unseen world, against mighty powers in this dark world, and against evil spirits in the heavenly places." Therefore, just because we are believers, we are not immune from the problems of life. We, too, get sick, have lean financial times, need encouragement, and face trials and tribulations that no one but God can bring us through. These dilemmas can drive us to our knees before Almighty God. Such was the case with the woman in today's study. She needed a higher power to do what man could not do.

CHAPTER 6

PART ONE

PRAYER
Always open the session with prayer and thanksgiving to God. Also include the Lesson Aim in your prayer.

INTRODUCTION
Introduce the chapter title and Scripture reference, including some background on the author of the book in which the Scripture is found, his audience, and his purpose for writing. (Note: Use a Bible Commentary, search online, or use your local library to get assistance). Then have a volunteer read the Key Verse aloud. It also appears at the beginning of each chapter in the student book. Now discuss the Key Verse and then have another volunteer read the Lesson Focus. Discuss. Finally introduce the vocabulary words or names and phrases listed in the Do You Know . . .? section, stressing their meaning.

CHAPTER REVIEW
After introducing the following topics, allow about five minutes to review and discuss Chapter 6.
- Why do desperate times call for desperate measures?
- Are believers ever desperate? When? Why? How?
- Who can we turn to when we are desperate?

DO YOU KNOW . . .?
To prepare for the lesson, study the following facts (all are further study for Chapter 6—"A Knee-Bent Healing").
- The disease that the woman had seemed incurable.
- The condition caused the woman to bleed constantly.
- It made her ritually unclean, excluding her from most social contact.
- The woman was desperate!
- Under Jewish law, if she touched Jesus, it would have made him unclean as well.
- The woman was considerate of Jesus. She reached out and touched His robe instead.
- The woman's faith caused her to be healed.

UP FRONT AND PERSONAL DISCUSSION QUESTIONS
After introducing and discussing the Up Front and Personal section of the book, go to the Up Front and Personal Discussion Questions in the student workbook. The workbook has space provided to record answers. Again, encourage participants to answer the questions as homework. If not, allow time for them to do so in class. To facilitate discussion, you might read them aloud, allow the participants to share their answers, and also share your thoughts. Always refer to the Bible as the final authority.

CHAPTER 6

PART TWO
SMALL GROUP STRATEGIES

Assemble Into Small Groups. Ask the participants to form small groups (tailor the number in each group to the size of the class). Assign each group a different section of the remaining parts of the chapter in the student book:
- Group #1   A Word from the Lord
- Group #2   Something to Think About. . .
- Group #3   A Doer of the Word

Also assign each group their respective sections in the student workbook (only A Word from the Lord and A Doer of the Word). Inform them that they are to complete and discuss the workbook questions for their respective section and report their answers to the larger group at the end of the study period.

Clock Watchers. Time constraints are very important in covering all the materials of the session. Therefore, approximately 15–20 minutes should be allotted for the Small Group Strategies.

Meditate and Debate. Encourage the small group to divide the questions and Scriptures among the members. Then, they should spend time discussing the answers to the questions.

Summary Reports. Each small group should prepare a summary of their session to share with the larger group by having a chairperson who will: (1) take notes; (2) summarize the discussion; and (3) present.

LARGE GROUP STRATEGIES

Reassemble. The groups should reassemble so that their findings can be discussed within the larger group.

Clock Watchers. Your objective is to cover all of the materials for each session. Therefore, allot two or three minutes for the small group spokespersons to give their summaries. In addition, allocate another two to three minutes to discuss the smaller groups' presentations.

A DOER OF THE WORD

Because it tells the participants how to apply God's Word to real-life situations, this is a very important part of your discussion. Therefore, summarize the salient points in this section and discuss them corporately.

Chapter 6

Something to Think About...
These questions can be used for further discussion sessions. The participants may ask additional questions, and more time for dialogue may be needed. You may want to designate another time for the questions to be discussed as a part of your class in the future or at another group study gathering.

Closing
Remind the participants to read Chapter 7 of *Living in the Excellence of Jesus!* and complete the exercises assigned in the student workbook. Also encourage them to bring their Bibles to each session. Always close with prayer.

UP FRONT AND PERSONAL DISCUSSION QUESTIONS
The answers will vary.
1. When sickness becomes a part of your family, name four ways that they respond. If you are the primary caretakers of one of them, what are your responsibilities, and how has this changed your life?

2. Know that sickness may lead to death, no matter how hard we pray. Are you prepared to deal with the financial, emotional, and spiritual issues that come with sickness and death? (Having a will, insurance or money—or access to money—for a funeral and the burial should already be in place.) If so, how are you prepared? If not, why not?

3. Staying healthy is important for a variety of reasons. How do you maintain your health?

4. If you know someone who has cancer, has had a heart attack, or has any other debilitating illness, how have you ministered to him/her or his/her family? If you have not, how can you minister?

A WORD FROM THE LORD
The answers will vary.
1. What type of disease do you think the woman had?

2. Discuss what emotions probably ran through the woman as she touched the hem of Jesus' robe.

3. Since she was isolated from society, how do you think the woman felt? Why?

4. Did the disciples ask a valid question when they asked Jesus why He had asked

them who touched Him being that there was such a large crowd? Why or why not?

5. Have you ever questioned Jesus? Share. What was His response to you? If you have not questioned Him, why not?

6. Paraphrase (state in your own words) and then personalize the following Scriptures on faith.
   a. Psalm 7:1, paraphrased and personalized
   b. Isaiah 12:2, paraphrased and personalized
   c. Matthew 12:21, paraphrased and personalized

SOMETHING TO THINK ABOUT. . .
The answers will vary.
1. Diseased, desperate, and delivered was the woman who was healed. She was an outcast and considered unclean by her community. Who are the unclean or the ignored members of your family, church, or neighborhood?

2. Is their status self-imposed and/or imposed by others? Explain.

3. Do you help to make a difference in their lives? If so, how?

A DOER OF THE WORD
The answers will vary.
1. To promote healthier eating and living, encourage all church groups to serve only healthy snacks and meals at church and leave out the red punch and red drinks. Discuss why you think the artificial preservatives and dyes in these drinks would be a concern for your health.

2. List the foods you have eaten over the last few days.

3. Would Jesus want to eat with you, and would He feel that you were eating a healthy meal? Why or why not?

4. If He came to your house or church for a meal or a snack, would you serve Jesus the food you ate? Why or why not?

CHAPTER 6

PRAYER FORUM
The answers will vary.

Write a prayer or words of inspiration asking God to help you make good decisions when choosing what foods to put in your body.

CHAPTER 7

AN EXPENSIVE MEAL

BASED ON DANIEL 1:5–12

Format for Sessions of 90 Minutes or More

PART ONE		PART TWO	
MIN.	**ACTIVITY**	**MIN.**	**ACTIVITY**
5	Prayer	20	Small Group Strategies
10	Introduction	15	Small Group Presentation
15	Chapter Review	15	Large Group Presentation
20	A Doer of the Word Discussion	5	Prayer Initiatives

To complete the group study in PART ONE and PART TWO, each participant will need a copy of the *Living in the Excellence of Jesus!* workbook that accompanies the student book. You may use PART ONE for sessions less than 90 minutes. Then, in the group settings, they will discuss their answers. Always close the sessions with prayer.

LESSON AIM: At the end of the one- or two-part session, the participants should: (1) know that there are many important choices to be made in this life and they will either negatively or positively impact our lives; (2) know that our eternal life is impacted by whether or not we choose Jesus (God's one and only Son) as our Lord and Savior; and (3) know that God does not force Himself on us; He loves us so much that He allows us to choose Him.

KEY VERSE: *"But Daniel was determined not to defile himself by eating the food and wine given to them by the king. He asked the chief of staff for permission not to eat these unacceptable foods"* (Daniel 1:8, NLT).

LESSON FOCUS: There are critical choices in life that believers have to make. We have to choose daily to obey and honor a Holy (set apart from sin) God. By our daily living, we must choose to reverence and bring glory to His name. When Daniel was taken away into captivity to Babylon as a young man, he and the three young assistants chose to honor God at all costs. The king's food and lifestyle were too expensive for them to indulge. We will explore how they walked with the Lord in a foreign land, when even their lives were at stake. God kept them and met their needs in the trouble. I pray that what we learn will inspire us to reach for excellence in serving our God, because indeed He is the Good Shepherd.

CHAPTER 7

PART ONE

PRAYER
Always open the session with prayer and thanksgiving to God. Also include the Lesson Aim in your prayer.

INTRODUCTION
Introduce the chapter title and Scripture reference, including some background on the author of the book in which the Scripture is found, his audience, and his purpose for writing. (Note: Use a Bible Commentary, search online, or use your local library to get assistance). Then have a volunteer read the Key Verse aloud. It also appears at the beginning of each chapter in the student book. Now discuss the Key Verse and then have another volunteer read the Lesson Focus. Discuss. Finally introduce the vocabulary words or names and phrases listed in the Do You Know . . .? section, stressing their meaning.

CHAPTER REVIEW
After introducing the following topics, allow about five minutes to review and discuss Chapter 7.
- What are some important choices that we have to make in life?
- What is the difference in how believers should make choices as opposed to nonbelievers?
- What happens if we make the wrong choice?

DO YOU KNOW . . .?
To prepare for the lesson, study the following facts (all are further study from Chapter 7—"An Expensive Meal").
- Even while Daniel and the three assistants were in bondage in Babylon for 70 years, a Sovereign God was still in control of world events.
- God is in control of His universe and never out of control.
- An all-powerful God will overcome evil with His good.
- Daniel and the three assistants were positive role models of dedication and commitment to a Holy God.
- We do not have to compromise our faith, even in a hostile environment.

UP FRONT AND PERSONAL DISCUSSION QUESTIONS
After introducing and discussing the Up Front and Personal section of the book, go to the Up Front and Personal Discussion Questions in the student workbook. The workbook has space provided to record answers. Again, encourage participants to answer the questions as homework. If not, allow time for them to do so in class. To facilitate discussion, you might read them aloud, allow the participants to share their answers, and also share your thoughts. Always refer to the Bible as the final authority.

PART TWO
SMALL GROUP STRATEGIES
Assemble Into Small Groups. Ask the participants to form small groups (tailor the number in each group to the size of the class). Assign each group a different section of the remaining parts of the chapter in the student book:
- Group #1   A Word from the Lord
- Group #2   Something to Think About. . .
- Group #3   A Doer of the Word

Also assign each group their respective sections in the student workbook (only A Word from the Lord and A Doer of the Word). Inform them that they are to complete and discuss the workbook questions for their respective section and report their answers to the larger group at the end of the study period.

Clock Watchers. Time constraints are very important in covering all the materials of the session. Therefore, approximately 15–20 minutes should be allotted for the Small Group Strategies.

Meditate and Debate. Encourage the small group to divide the questions and Scriptures among the members. Then, they should spend time discussing the answers to the questions.

Summary Reports. Each small group should prepare a summary of their session to share with the larger group by having a chairperson who will: (1) take notes; (2) summarize the discussion; and (3) present.

LARGE GROUP STRATEGIES
Reassemble. The groups should reassemble so that their findings can be discussed within the larger group.

Clock Watchers. Your objective is to cover all of the materials for each session. Therefore, allot two or three minutes for the small group spokespersons to give their summaries. In addition, allocate another two to three minutes to discuss the smaller groups' presentations.

A DOER OF THE WORD
Because it tells the participants how to apply God's Word to real-life situations, this is a very important part of your discussion. Therefore, summarize the salient points in this section and discuss them corporately.

Chapter 7

SOMETHING TO THINK ABOUT. . .
These questions can be used for further discussion sessions. The participants may ask additional questions, and more time for dialogue may be needed. You may want to designate another time for the questions to be discussed as a part of your class in the future or at another group study gathering.

CLOSING
Remind the participants to read Chapter 8 of *Living in the Excellence of Jesus!* and complete the exercises assigned in the student workbook. Also encourage them to bring their Bibles to each session. Always close with prayer.

UP FRONT AND PERSONAL DISCUSSION QUESTIONS
The answers will vary.

1. The "Genesis" family knew how to love and share what they had with others. How does your church and biological families share love with others?

2. Write a news article that describes how you would have rewritten the ending of this story.

3. Describe your favorite family event from your childhood or from today. Think about how you laughed, or ate your favorite food, or listened to the "family history."

4. Share your tradition for holidays or any other special time.

A WORD FROM THE LORD
The answers will vary.

1. Why was Daniel able to stay focused and committed to his diet?

2. If you struggle/have struggled with food or any other form of addiction, how do you/did you stay focused on how not to participate in whatever it was that could harm you?

3. Write and speak the names of the young Hebrew men before they were changed. Should we honor their translated Hebrew names or only say the "new" names given to them? Why? Why not?

4. God often sends a "ram in the bush" to help us when we are held prisoner in various ways. Daniel and the other men had a "ram in the bush." Who was he and who has been your "ram in the bush"? Explain.

5. Paraphrase (state in your own words) and then personalize the following Scriptures on faith.
   a. Mark 2:5, paraphrased and personalized
   b. Romans 2:7, paraphrased and personalized
   c. 1 Timothy 6:11, paraphrased and personalized

SOMETHING TO THINK ABOUT. . .
The answers will vary.

1. Who are the people you most admire for taking a stand for justice and why?

2. Describe a time you took a stand for justice.

3. What were the results, and who helped you in your quest for justice?

A DOER OF THE WORD
The answers will vary.

1. Fasting and prayer are two ways to prepare ourselves for service for the Lord. Select one food or drink item that you will give up for 30 days. Also, select a behavior or thought you will not give in to for 30 days. Feel free to keep a journal in words or pictures to share about your 30-day journey. When will you begin your fast?

2. Designate a particular time of day to pray for strength to sustain you and your classmates. You may want to select a prayer partner during the next 30 days. You can check on and pray for each other once a week or every day.

PRAYER FORUM
The answers will vary.

Write a prayer or words of inspiration asking God to help you walk in His principles and honor Him, even when life seems impossible.

CHAPTER 8

TROUBLE IN THE CAMP

BASED ON JOSHUA 6:16–21; 7:1, 10–13, 20–21

Format for Sessions of 90 Minutes or More

PART ONE

MIN.	ACTIVITY
5	Prayer
10	Introduction
15	Chapter Review
20	A Doer of the Word Discussion

PART TWO

MIN.	ACTIVITY
20	Small Group Strategies
15	Small Group Presentation
15	Large Group Presentation
5	Prayer Initiatives

To complete the group study in PART ONE and PART TWO, each participant will need a copy of the *Living in the Excellence of Jesus!* workbook that accompanies the student book. You may use PART ONE for sessions less than 90 minutes. Then, in the group settings, they will discuss their answers. Always close the sessions with prayer.

LESSON AIM: At the end of the one- or two-part session, the participants should: (1) know Almighty God has a standard and He expects all believers to obey His commands; (2) know obedience is not optional; (3) know obedience is better than sacrifice; and (4) know there is a harsh penalty for disobeying God.

KEY VERSE: *"But Israel violated the instructions about the things set apart for the LORD. A man named Achan had stolen some of these dedicated things, so the LORD was very angry with the Israelites. Achan was the son of Carmi, a descendant of Zimri son of Zerah, of the tribe of Judah"* (Joshua 7:1, NLT).

LESSON FOCUS: God desires obedience from those who are called by His name. Part of believers' worship of a Holy God is to obey His commands. This lesson focuses on the consequences of disobedience. God specifically spelled out how the battle of Jericho was to be fought to His chosen people (the Israelites). He was leading in the fight and was going to bring the victory. He gave the Israelites the charge to obey His edicts to the letter. Therefore, when Achan chose to disobey, Achan brought trouble into the Israelites' camp. The consequences were death to him and his entire family. We, too, bring trouble into our own lives as well as those of others when we disobey an all-knowing, all-present, and all-powerful God. Others are either blessed or suffer because of the choices we make. Clearly, we should choose to obey God.

Chapter 8

PART ONE

Prayer

Always open the session with prayer and thanksgiving to God. Also include the Lesson Aim in your prayer.

Introduction

Introduce the chapter title and Scripture reference, including some background on the author of the book in which the Scripture is found, his audience, and his purpose for writing. (Note: Use a Bible Commentary, search online, or use your local library to get assistance). Then have a volunteer read the Key Verse aloud. It also appears at the beginning of each chapter in the student book. Now discuss the Key Verse and then have another volunteer read the Lesson Focus. Discuss. Finally introduce the vocabulary words or names and phrases listed in the Do You Know . . .? section, stressing their meaning.

Chapter Review

After introducing the following topics, allow about five minutes to review and discuss Chapter 8.

- What do we mean when we say "God is holy"?
- What is God's standard?
- Why does God demand obedience?
- What can happen when we are unfaithful to God?

Do You Know . . .?

To prepare for the lesson, study the following names, phrases, and definitions. Match the words to the phrases that describe them (all are taken from Chapter 8—"Trouble in the Camp").

1. Achan
2. Joshua
3. Rahab
4. sacred
5. "the Lord's treasury"
6. "the Valley of Trouble"
7. unfaithful

a. possessions that God deemed should be set aside for Him
b. a monument commemorating the killing of Achan and his family
c. disloyal, disobedient
d. thief, disobedient to God's commands
e. the prostitute in Jericho, who helped the two spies sent by Joshua to spy out the land
f. set apart for God
g. Moses successor, led the Children of Israel into the Promised Land (Canaan)

Answers:
1. d
2. g
3. e
4. f or a
5. a or f
6. b
7. c

Up Front and Personal Discussion Questions

After introducing and discussing the Up Front and Personal section of the book, go to the Up Front and Personal Discussion Questions in the student workbook. The workbook has space provided to record answers. Again, encourage participants to answer the questions as homework. If not, allow time for them to do so in class. To facilitate discussion, you might read them aloud, allow the participants to share their answers, and also share your thoughts. Always refer to the Bible as the final authority.

PART TWO
Small Group Strategies

Assemble Into Small Groups. Ask the participants to form small groups (tailor the number in each group to the size of the class). Assign each group a different section of the remaining parts of the chapter in the student book:

- Group #1   A Word from the Lord
- Group #2   Something to Think About...
- Group #3   A Doer of the Word

Also assign each group their respective sections in the student workbook (only A Word from the Lord and A Doer of the Word). Inform them that they are to complete and discuss the workbook questions for their respective section and report their answers to the larger group at the end of the study period.

Clock Watchers. Time constraints are very important in covering all the materials of the session. Therefore, approximately 15–20 minutes should be allotted for the Small Group Strategies.

Meditate and Debate. Encourage the small group to divide the questions and Scriptures among the members. Then, they should spend time discussing the answers to the questions.

Summary Reports. Each small group should prepare a summary of their session to share with the larger group by having a chairperson who will: (1) take notes; (2) summarize the discussion; and (3) present.

LARGE GROUP STRATEGIES

Reassemble. The groups should reassemble so that their findings can be discussed within the larger group.

Clock Watchers. Your objective is to cover all of the materials for each session. Therefore, allot two or three minutes for the small group spokespersons to give their summaries. In addition, allocate another two to three minutes to discuss the smaller groups' presentations.

A DOER OF THE WORD

Because it tells the participants how to apply God's Word to real-life situations, this is a very important part of your discussion. Therefore, summarize the salient points in this section and discuss them corporately.

SOMETHING TO THINK ABOUT. . .

These questions can be used for further discussion sessions. The participants may ask additional questions, and more time for dialogue may be needed. You may want to designate another time for the questions to be discussed as a part of your class in the future or at another group study gathering.

CLOSING

Remind the participants to read Chapter 9 of *Living in the Excellence of Jesus!* and complete the exercises assigned in the student workbook. Also encourage them to bring their Bibles to each session. Always close with prayer.

UP FRONT AND PERSONAL DISCUSSION QUESTIONS
The answers will vary.

1. Write your ending to the Marcus story and how you think the family reacted to his death.

2. What was your initial thought as to what made Marcus slightly different?

3. After examining your own family, share some thoughts on the different personalities and roles that each person plays. Where do you fit in and how do you see yourself?

4. Name three positive characteristics about your family as a whole.

A WORD FROM THE LORD
The answers will vary.
1. Why do you think Achan wanted to steal the treasures that were to be dedicated to the Lord's house?

2. Do you think in Achan's case, the punishment fit the crime? Why or why not?

3. If someone from your family commits a crime, do you think the entire family should pay? Give examples to support your belief.

4. Do you think crime or godly ways would be different if the entire family had to pay very stiff penalties (i.e., monetary fines, shame, jail time) for one member's criminal behavior or ungodly behavior in the church?

5. What is your definition of "godly" or "ungodly" behavior?

6. What were the repercussions that you experienced when doing what the Lord did not want you to do?

7. What were the treasures that Achan stole and why were they important to the Lord's treasury?

8. Discuss why Joshua was an excellent leader.

9. What were some of the difficulties and rewards he faced as a leader of ex-slaves?

10. Share your understanding of why the number seven is a number of significance within the Judea-Christian faith.

11. Paraphrase (state in your own words) and then personalize the following Scriptures on faith.
    a. Genesis 2:16–17, paraphrased and personalized
    b. Matthew 5:20, paraphrased and personalized
    c. 1 John 2:6, paraphrased and personalized

CHAPTER 8

SOMETHING TO THINK ABOUT...
The answers will vary.

1. Achan stole from the treasury of the Lord. Are Christians ever guilty of stealing from the Lord? Explain.

2. Name three ways that you think Christians steal from the Lord.

3. List different ways that maybe you need to give back to God on a daily basis.

A DOER OF THE WORD
The answers will vary.

1. List three social programs that your church is actively participating in financially and with people and/or supply power.

2. Do you think Jesus wants us involved with passing laws and regulations to help provide better health care for all Americans? Why or why not?

3. If you believe that justice should impact all aspects of our lives, how do you see Christians as change agents in your particular community and in the world?

4. What are your doing personally and collectively to make justice a major focus in your life and the lives of others?

PRAYER FORUM
The answers will vary.

Write a prayer or words of inspiration asking God to help you be obedient to His Word so that you can walk in the excellence of God.

CHAPTER 9

WORKING HARD OR HARDLY WORKING?

BASED ON NEHEMIAH 1:3–4; 4:1–9; 5:15–16

Format for Sessions of 90 Minutes or More

PART ONE

MIN.	ACTIVITY
5	Prayer
10	Introduction
15	Chapter Review
20	A Doer of the Word Discussion

PART TWO

MIN.	ACTIVITY
20	Small Group Strategies
15	Small Group Presentation
15	Large Group Presentation
5	Prayer Initiatives

To complete the group study in PART ONE and PART TWO, each participant will need a copy of the *Living in the Excellence of Jesus!* workbook that accompanies the student book. You may use PART ONE for sessions less than 90 minutes. Then, in the group settings, they will discuss their answers. Always close the sessions with prayer.

LESSON AIM: At the end of the one- or two-part session, the participants should: (1) know God does not save us to sit on our seats of "do nothing"; (2) know He desires for us to help work in building His kingdom so that we can help win other lost souls to Christ; (3) believe God can use ordinary people to do extraordinary things in His kingdom-building initiative; and (4) know that the time to work for God is now.

KEY VERSE: *"At last the wall was completed to half its height around the entire city, for the people had worked with enthusiasm"* (Nehemiah 4:6, NLT).

LESSON FOCUS: Our focus is on the call of God. God wants vessels He can use to be workers to help repair the broken temples and walls of people's wasted lives. He wants workers to go to the highways and byways and be witnesses for Him—to help build His kingdom. Even though Nehemiah was a common man, exiled in a foreign land, and serving as a cupbearer to the Persian king Artaxerxes, he was still not out of God's reach. In fact, a Sovereign God (one who is in control and never out of control) called Nehemiah to return to Jerusalem, his home, and rebuild the temple and walls that lay in waste from the time their capturers destroyed them and took many of their young men into captivity, including Daniel. Nehemiah shows us today how to walk in excellence before a Holy God because God called him and he answered.

CHAPTER 9

PART ONE

PRAYER
Always open the session with prayer and thanksgiving to God. Also include the Lesson Aim in your prayer.

INTRODUCTION
Introduce the chapter title and Scripture reference, including some background on the author of the book in which the Scripture is found, his audience, and his purpose for writing. (Note: Use a Bible Commentary, search online, or use your local library to get assistance). Then have a volunteer read the Key Verse aloud. It also appears at the beginning of each chapter in the student book. Now discuss the Key Verse and then have another volunteer read the Lesson Focus. Discuss. Finally introduce the vocabulary words or names and phrases listed in the Do You Know . . .? section, stressing their meaning.

CHAPTER REVIEW
After introducing the following topics, allow about five minutes to review and discuss Chapter 9.
- Does God call to willing vessels that He can use for His glory?
- Do we hear the voice of God calling?
- Are we open to God's lead?

DO YOU KNOW...?
To prepare for the lesson, study the following facts (all are further study for Chapter 9—"Working Hard or Hardly Working?").
- As an exile in a foreign land, Nehemiah was subject to King Artaxerxes.
- Even though the Israelites had been in bondage to the Babylonians for approximately 70 years, Jerusalem's walls were still in ruin from the battle.
- Nehemiah was to lead the third expedition of freed Israelites back to their homeland.
- Nehemiah was not only a man of character, but one of persistence and prayer, even in a foreign land.
- Because of Nehemiah's dedication, persistence, and prayer, the wall was built in 52 days.
- Even in captivity, Nehemiah did not give up on His God.

UP FRONT AND PERSONAL DISCUSSION QUESTIONS
After introducing and discussing the Up Front and Personal section of the book, go to the Up Front and Personal Discussion Questions in the student workbook. The workbook has space provided to record answers. Again, encourage participants to answer the questions as homework. If not, allow time for them to do so in class. To

facilitate discussion, you might read them aloud, allow the participants to share their answers, and also share your thoughts. Always refer to the Bible as the final authority.

PART TWO
SMALL GROUP STRATEGIES
Assemble Into Small Groups. Ask the participants to form small groups (tailor the number in each group to the size of the class). Assign each group a different section of the remaining parts of the chapter in the student book:
- Group #1   A Word from the Lord
- Group #2   Something to Think About. . .
- Group #3   A Doer of the Word

Also assign each group their respective sections in the student workbook (only A Word from the Lord and A Doer of the Word). Inform them that they are to complete and discuss the workbook questions for their respective section and report their answers to the larger group at the end of the study period.

Clock Watchers. Time constraints are very important in covering all the materials of the session. Therefore, approximately 15–20 minutes should be allotted for the Small Group Strategies.

Meditate and Debate. Encourage the small group to divide the questions and Scriptures among the members. Then, they should spend time discussing the answers to the questions.

Summary Reports. Each small group should prepare a summary of their session to share with the larger group by having a chairperson who will: (1) take notes; (2) summarize the discussion, and (3) present.

LARGE GROUP STRATEGIES
Reassemble. The groups should reassemble so that their findings can be discussed within the larger group.

Clock Watchers. Your objective is to cover all of the materials for each session. Therefore, allot two or three minutes for the small group spokespersons to give their summaries. In addition, allocate another two to three minutes to discuss the smaller groups' presentations.

Chapter 9

A Doer of the Word
Because it tells the participants how to apply God's Word to real-life situations, this is a very important part of your discussion. Therefore, summarize the salient points in this section and discuss them corporately.

Something to Think About. . .
These questions can be used for further discussion sessions. The participants may ask additional questions, and more time for dialogue may be needed. You may want to designate another time for the questions to be discussed as a part of your class in the future or at another group study gathering.

Closing
Remind the participants to read Chapter 10 of *Living in the Excellence of Jesus!* and complete the exercises assigned in the student workbook. Also encourage them to bring their Bibles to each session. Always close with prayer.

UP FRONT AND PERSONAL DISCUSSION QUESTIONS
The answers will vary.

1. Share memories you may personally have or someone you know may have in experiencing racism, sexism, etc.

2. What are some of the benefits for those who marched in various protest marches during the 1950s through 2000s (war protests included)?

3. Name one or two people today who have made valuable contributions to your life. Share what they have done that you are grateful for.

4. Now write a "thank-you" note to the two people who have blessed you so much.

A WORD FROM THE LORD
The answers will vary.

1. What are some of the character traits that Nehemiah possessed that helped him to stay strong in the work of the Lord even under extreme opposition?

2. Why did the leaders not want Nehemiah and the other workers to complete the building of the wall?

3. What is your response to naysayers in the church or for progressive movement for justice in the community or the church?

4. Recount a time when you were opposed to being supportive of someone who

CHAPTER 9

wanted to do something that you thought should not be done (i.e., helping someone else in their time of need), but he/she made the best choice.

5. How did you respond during and after the completion of the task recounted in number 4?

6. Paraphrase (state in your own words) and then personalize the following Scriptures on faith.
   a. Matthew 9:37–38, paraphrased and personalized
   b. Luke 10:3, paraphrased and personalized
   c. John 21:15, paraphrased and personalized

SOMETHING TO THINK ABOUT. . .
The answers will vary.
1. Nehemiah took a stand to build the wall in spite of the taunts and teasing from others. His faith, hard work, and the contributions of others paid off and the wall was built. Think about a time that you gave up before you finished a project and a time when you stayed with a project regardless of what others said and it paid off. Share.

2. Describe why you gave up and why you hung in there.

3. What Scriptures, songs, or people come to mind that gave you a sense of strength and the hope to keep trying?

A DOER OF THE WORD
The answers will vary.
1. When is faith an obstacle and when is it a blessing? (You can define the word *faith* as having faith in God or faith in whatever you want to.)

2. List programs and/or relationships that you built in your lifetime that others have supported or worked against. Why did others support or not support your work?

3. Write out a covenant with the Lord on giving excellent service and work to a particular project that you desire to complete. Include a time limit.

PRAYER FORUM
The answers will vary.
Write a prayer or words of inspiration asking God to help you be in tune to His call upon your life and move you to excellence in your worship of Him.

Chapter 10

ROI: A RETURN ON INVESTMENT

BASED ON MATTHEW 25:14–26, 28

Format for Sessions of 90 Minutes or More

PART ONE			**PART TWO**	
MIN.	**ACTIVITY**		**MIN.**	**ACTIVITY**
5	Prayer		20	Small Group Strategies
10	Introduction		15	Small Group Presentation
15	Chapter Review		15	Large Group Presentation
20	A Doer of the Word Discussion		5	Prayer Initiatives

To complete the group study in PART ONE and PART TWO, each participant will need a copy of the *Living in the Excellence of Jesus!* workbook that accompanies the student book. You may use PART ONE for sessions less than 90 minutes. Then, in the group settings, they will discuss their answers. Always close the sessions with prayer.

LESSON AIM: At the end of the one- or two-part session, the participants should: (1) know God has given all of us talents (abilities) and time that we are to use to His honor and glory; (2) see that He expects us to use His gifts, on loan to us, to help build His kingdom; (3) believe He expects us to use His gifts wisely; and (4) know He expects a good return on what He has invested in us.

KEY VERSE: *"The servant to whom he had entrusted the five bags of silver came forward with five more and said, 'Master, you gave me five bags of silver to invest, and I have earned five more.' 'The master was full of praise. "Well done, my good and faithful servant. You have been faithful in handling this small amount, so now I will give you many more responsibilities. Let's celebrate together!"'"* (Matthew 25:20–21, NLT).

LESSON FOCUS: The investments that God has made in us are very important to Him. Our focus this session will be on using our time and talents wisely and to Almighty God's glory. Therefore, we need to go to Him in prayer and find out what His will is for our lives and pursue walking in His will. In order to achieve excellence in our worship of a very deserving God, we must let Him lead us into bringing an excellent return on what He has entrusted to us.

PART ONE

Prayer
Always open the session with prayer and thanksgiving to God. Also include the Lesson Aim in your prayer.

Introduction
Introduce the chapter title and Scripture reference, including some background on the author of the book in which the Scripture is found, his audience, and his purpose for writing. (Note: Use a Bible Commentary, search online, or use your local library to get assistance). Then have a volunteer read the Key Verse aloud. It also appears at the beginning of each chapter in the student book. Now discuss the Key Verse and then have another volunteer read the Lesson Focus. Discuss. Finally introduce the vocabulary words or names and phrases listed in the Do You Know . . .? section, stressing their meaning.

Chapter Review
After introducing the following topics, allow about five minutes to review and discuss Chapter 10.
- Do you know what talent(s) God has entrusted to you?
- Are you using your talent(s) wisely?
- Are you using your talent(s) to God's glory?
- What have you done for God lately?

Do You Know. . . ?
To prepare for the lesson, study the following words and definitions (all are taken from Chapter 10—"ROI: A Return on Investment").
entrusted—a possession given in the care of someone else
faithful servant—one who uses his/her talent(s) and time wisely (to the glory of God)
lazy servant—one who does not use his/her talent(s) and time wisely (to the glory of God)
ROI: A Return on Investment—the profit after all the expenses are paid
servant—one who serves; God considers all believers servants to Him and humanity
the kingdom of God—presently it reigns in all believers' hearts because we have accepted Jesus Christ as our Lord and personal Savior; all believers will reign with Jesus on the new Earth that is to come
the rich master—the rich master in the story represents God

Up Front and Personal Discussion Questions
After introducing and discussing the Up Front and Personal section of the book, go to the Up Front and Personal Discussion Questions in the student workbook. The

CHAPTER 10

workbook has space provided to record answers. Again, encourage participants to answer the questions as homework. If not, allow time for them to do so in class. To facilitate discussion, you might read them aloud, allow the participants to share their answers, and also share your thoughts. Always refer to the Bible as the final authority.

PART TWO
SMALL GROUP STRATEGIES
Assemble Into Small Groups. Ask the participants to form small groups (tailor the number in each group to the size of the class). Assign each group a different section of the remaining parts of the chapter in the student book:
- Group #1   A Word from the Lord
- Group #2   Something to Think About
- Group #3   A Doer of the Word

Also assign each group their respective sections in the student workbook (only A Word from the Lord and A Doer of the Word). Inform them that they are to complete and discuss the workbook questions for their respective section and report their answers to the larger group at the end of the study period.

Clock Watchers. Time constraints are very important in covering all the materials of the session. Therefore, approximately 15–20 minutes should be allotted for the Small Group Strategies.

Meditate and Debate. Encourage the small group to divide the questions and Scriptures among the members. Then, they should spend time discussing the answers to the questions.

Summary Reports. Each small group should prepare a summary of their session to share with the larger group by having a chairperson who will: (1) take notes; (2) summarize the discussion; and (3) present.

LARGE GROUP STRATEGIES
Reassemble. The groups should reassemble so that their findings can be discussed within the larger group.

Clock Watchers. Your objective is to cover all of the materials for each session. Therefore, allot two or three minutes for the small group spokespersons to give their summaries. In addition, allocate another two to three minutes to discuss the smaller groups' presentations.

Chapter 10

A Doer of the Word
Because it tells the participants how to apply God's Word to real-life situations, this is a very important part of your discussion. Therefore, summarize the salient points in this section and discuss them corporately.

Something to Think About...
These questions can be used for further discussion sessions. The participants may ask additional questions, and more time for dialogue may be needed. You may want to designate another time for the questions to be discussed as a part of your class in the future or at another group study gathering.

Closing
Help the participants to recall some of the principles that they have learned from chapters 1–10 of the *Living in the Excellence of Jesus!* books. Remind them that believers are to obey God's Word by being doers of what He has called us to do. Also encourage them to read their Bibles daily. Always close with prayer.

UP FRONT AND PERSONAL DISCUSSION QUESTIONS
The answers will vary.

1. Describe a time when you thought your own accomplishments were due to your efforts and no one else's.

2. Is the thinking in number one good or hurtful? Why or why not?

3. Do you know of anyone who believes that pulling him/herself up by his/her own bootstraps is realistic? Share.

4. What would be another word or phrase to use in place of boots and bootstraps when discussing self-help?

5. Discuss what it means to work together individually and collectively for the Lord and if both or one way is better than the other. Give examples to support your beliefs.

A WORD FROM THE LORD

1. Explain how this story makes you feel about the Master (God)?

2. Reread the explanation of the servant who was given the one talent as to why he did not invest the money. Discuss his response and how it applied then and does or does not apply today?

3. What do you think the servant, who did not invest, is saying in regards to his actions?

4. Do you think that the first two servants wanted to invest the money so they could be free and have their own investment firms, or freedom to do what they wanted? Why or why not?

5. Paraphrase (state in your own words) and personalize the following Scriptures on working for God.
   a. John 15:1–2, paraphrased and personalized
   b. John 15:4, paraphrased and personalized
   c. John 15:7, paraphrased and personalized

SOMETHING TO THINK ABOUT. . .
The answers will vary.
1. Jesus has a way of asking questions that address the real problem in our lives? How would you respond to Jesus' question, "Do you want to be healed?" What do you need to be healed from today?

2. Is education the key to success at all times? What forms of education do we need to have to be successful in life? Explain.

3. Is Carter G. Woodson's "back door mentality" of control true today? Why? Why not?

4. Discuss ways to change the back door mentality way of thinking and living.

A DOER OF THE WORD
The answers will vary.
1. Describe the after-school programs in your church. Who is responsible for the program? Are science and math a part of these programs?

2. Do you think that math and science are a part of the Scriptures? Share your reasons why or why not. Use Scriptures to support your answer.

3. What does the word *education* mean to you? How important is education to you, your family, and your church? Share how important you think education is to the African American people.

Chapter 10

PRAYER FORUM
The answers will vary.
> Write a prayer or words of inspiration asking God for help in bringing in a good return on His investment in you.

Notes

Notes